NATIONAL GEOGRAPHIC

Legs

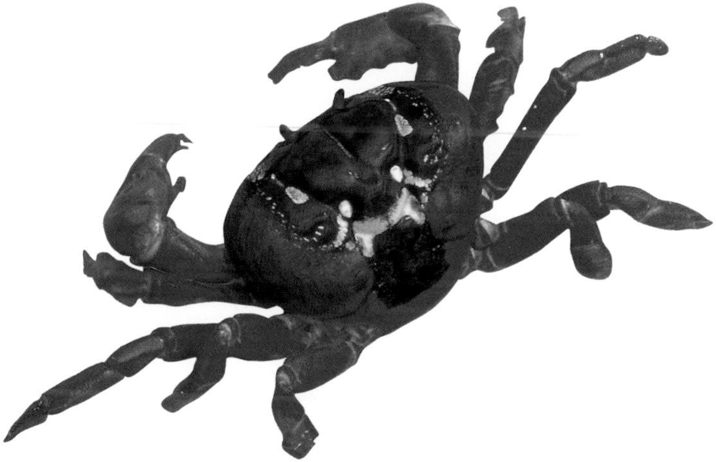

Thea Hutt

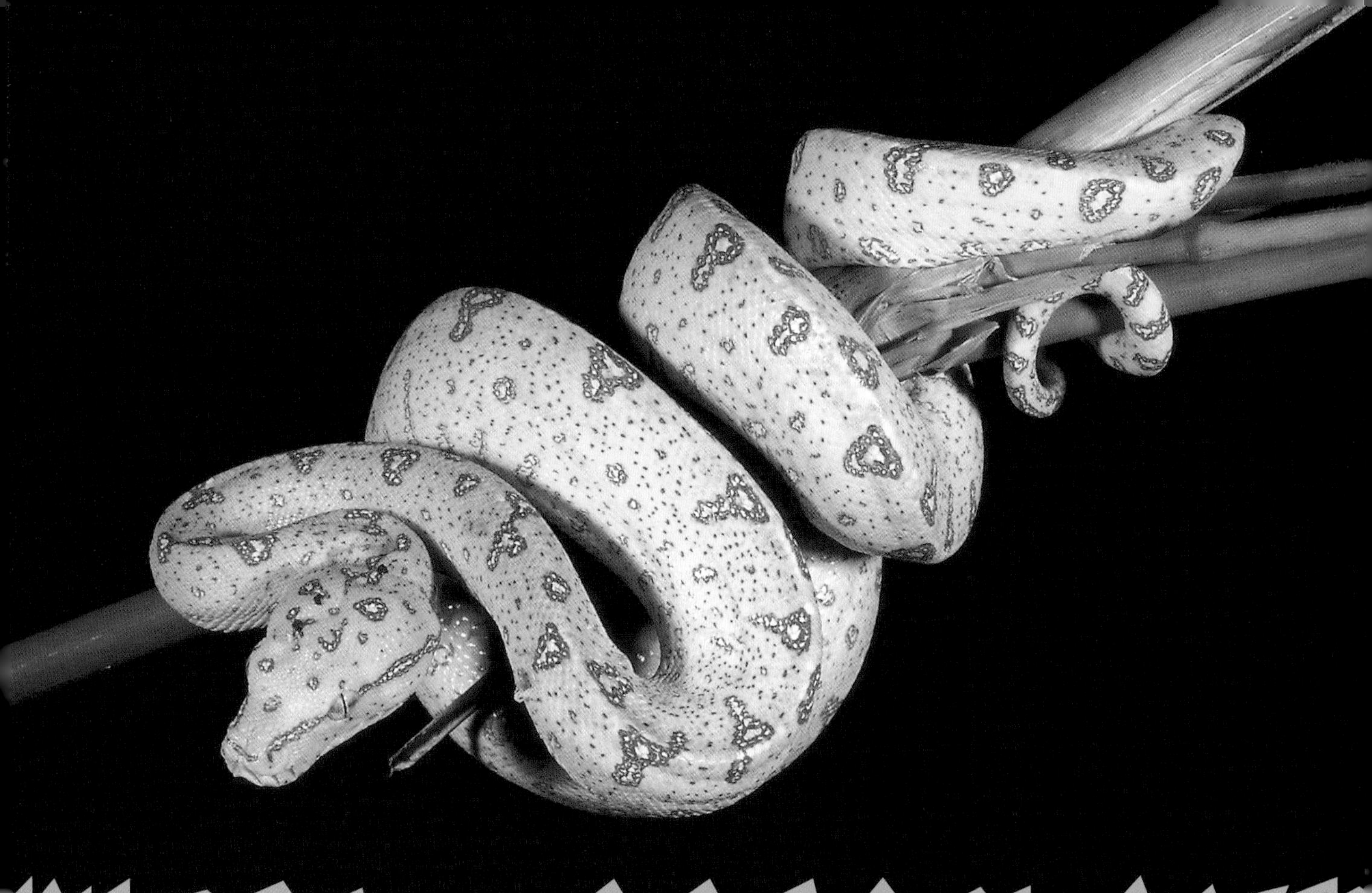

A snake has zero legs.

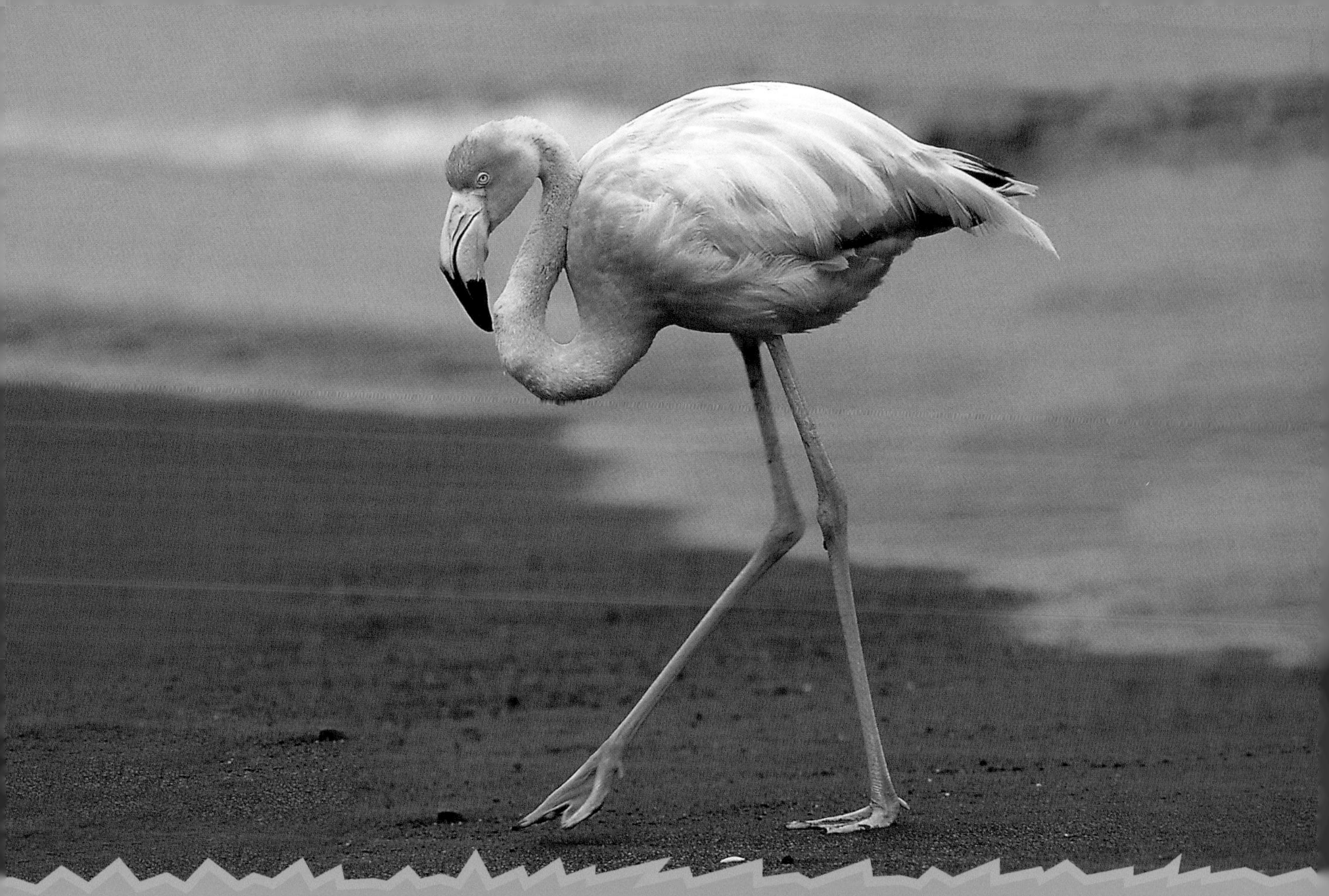

A bird has two legs.

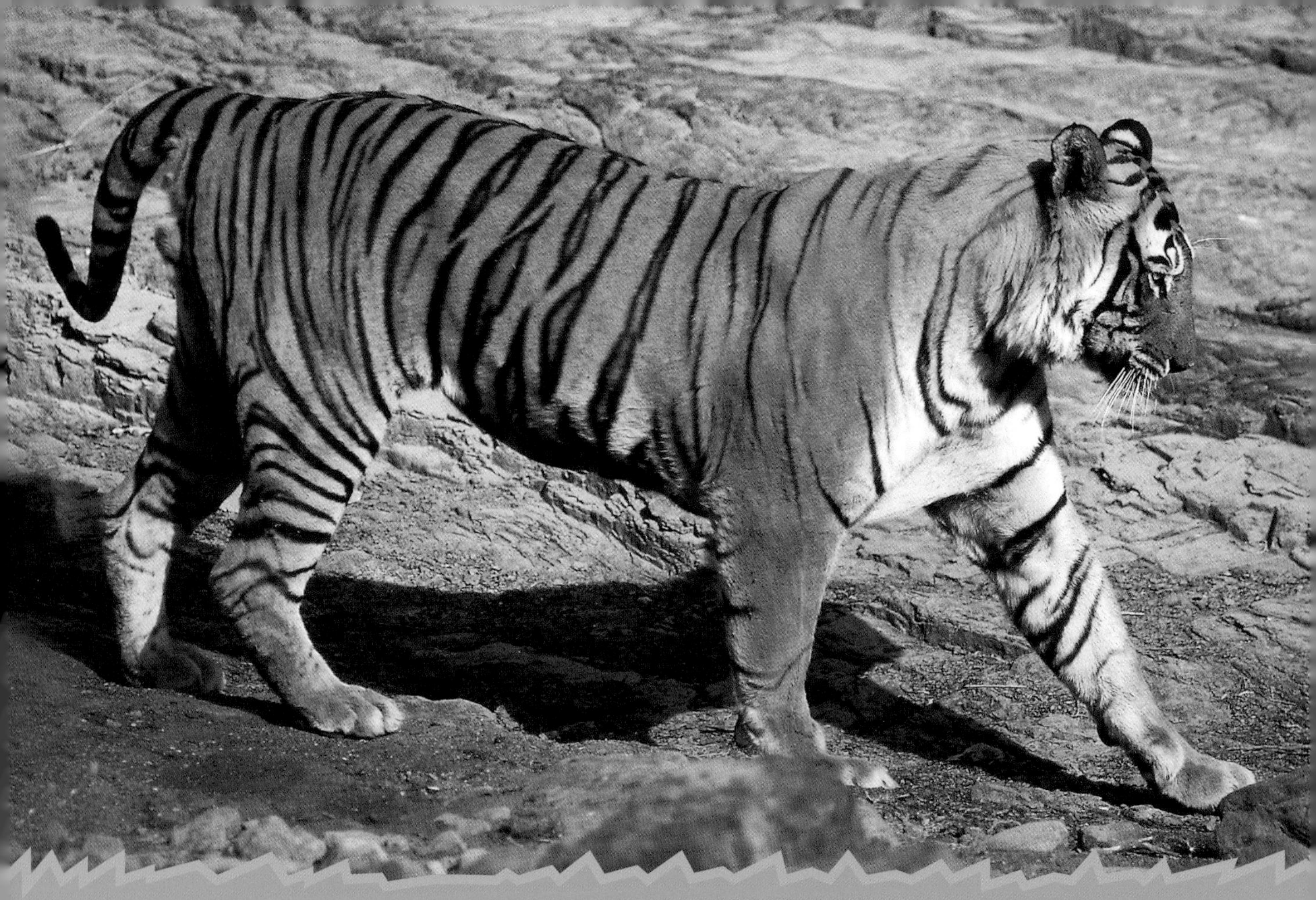

A tiger has four legs.

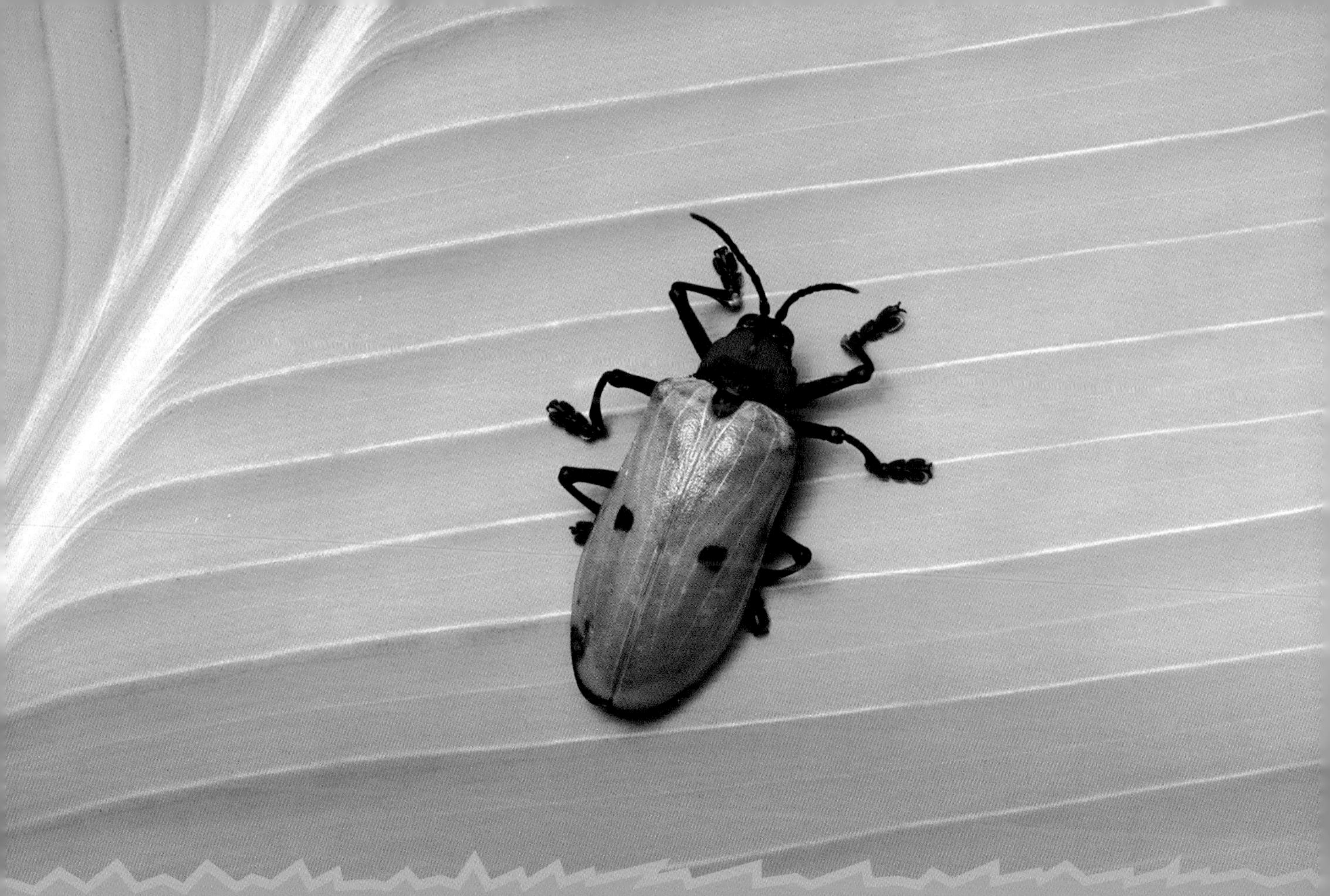

A beetle has six legs.

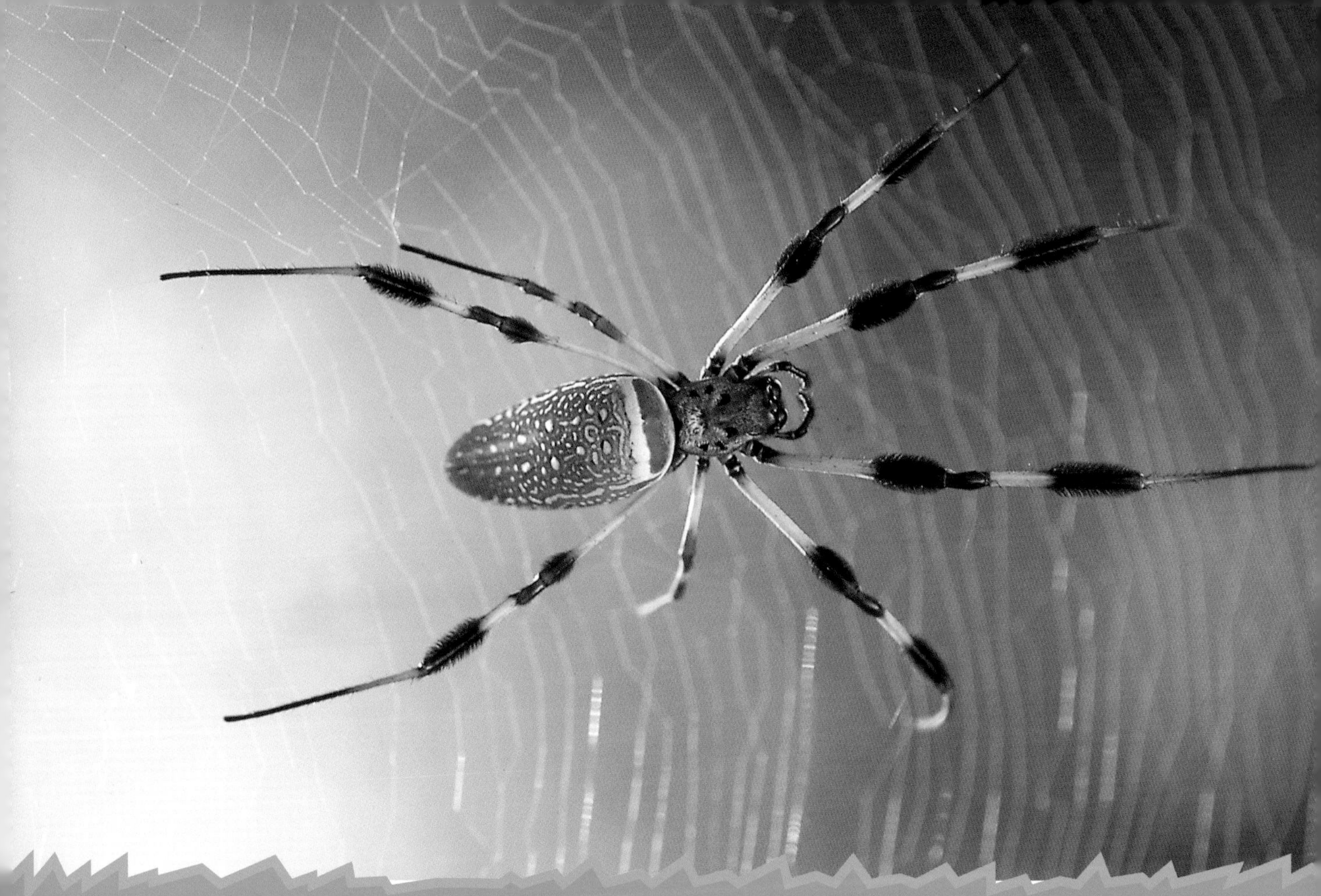

A spider has eight legs.

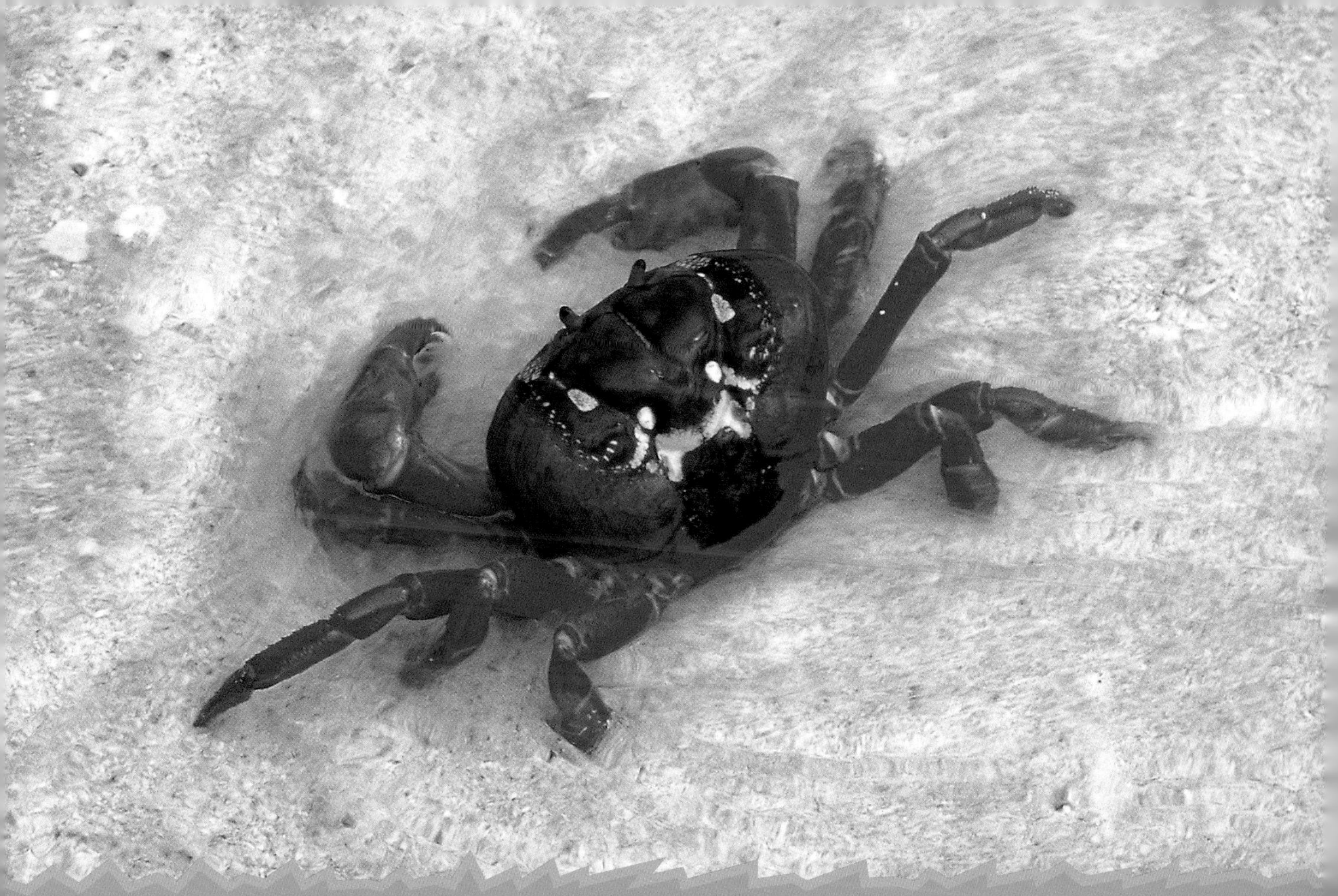

A crab has ten legs.

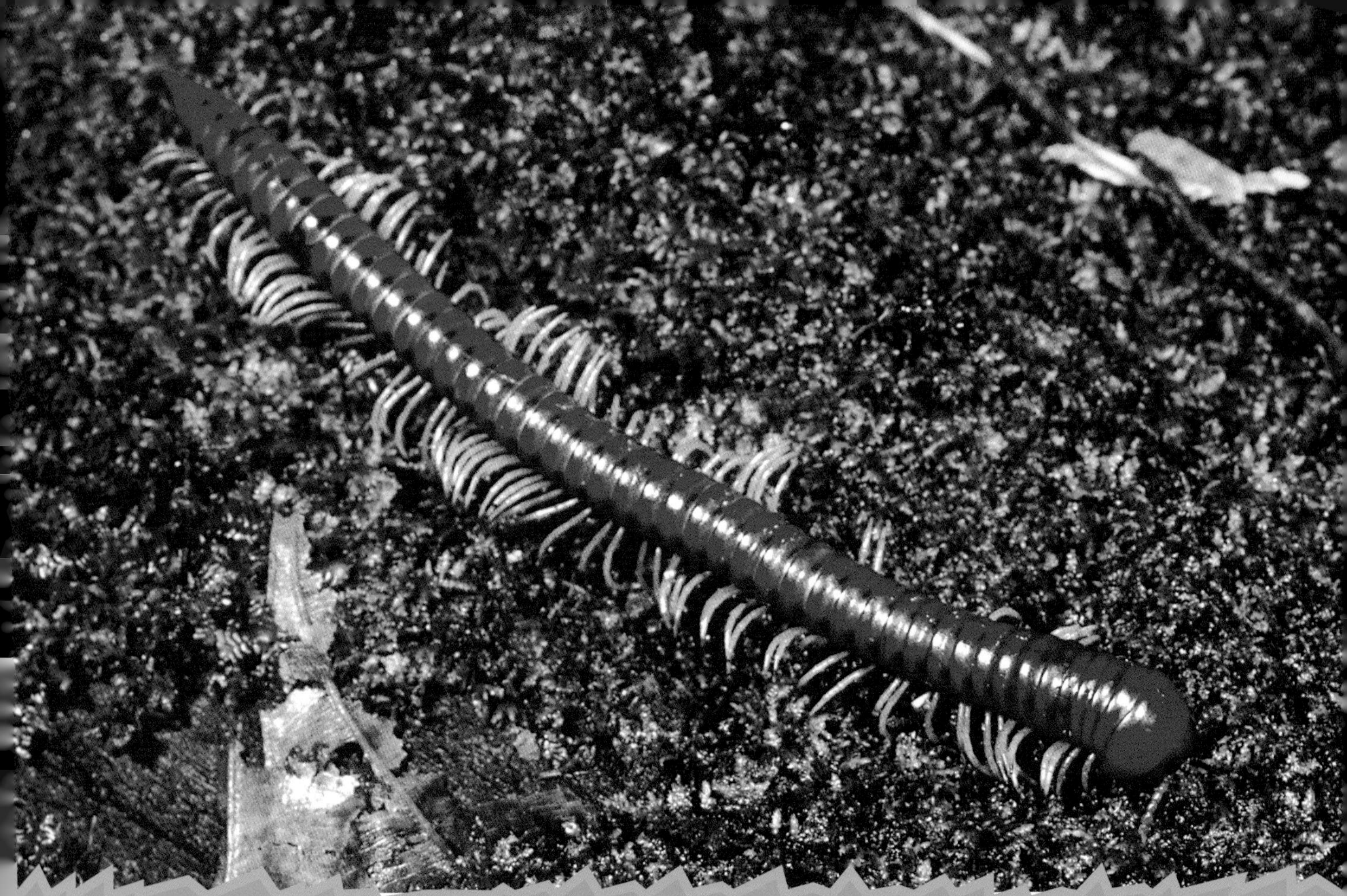

A millipede has *lots* of legs.